PHP
QUICKSTART GUIDE

The Simplified Beginner's Guide To PHP

ClydeBank
TECHNOLOGY

Copyright 2015 by ClydeBank Media - All Rights Reserved.

This document is geared towards providing exact and reliable information in regards to the topic and issue covered. The publication is sold with the idea that the publisher is not required to render accounting, officially permitted, or otherwise, qualified services. If advice is necessary, legal or professional, a practiced individual in the profession should be ordered.

From a Declaration of Principles which was accepted and approved equally by a Committee of the American Bar Association and a Committee of Publishers and Associations. In no way is it legal to reproduce, duplicate, or transmit any part of this document in either electronic means or in printed format. Recording of this publication is strictly prohibited and any storage of this document is not allowed unless with written permission from the publisher.

The information provided herein is stated to be truthful and consistent, in that any liability, in terms of inattention or otherwise, by any usage or abuse of any policies, processes, or directions contained within is the solitary and utter responsibility of the recipient reader. Under no circumstances will any legal responsibility or blame be held against the publisher for any reparation, damages, or monetary loss due to the information herein, either directly or indirectly. Respective authors own all copyrights not held by the publisher. The information herein is offered for informational purposes solely, and is universal as so. The presentation of the information is without contract or any type of guarantee assurance.

Trademarks: All trademarks are the property of their respective owners. The trademarks that are used are without any consent, and the publication of the trademark is without permission or backing by the trademark owner. All trademarks and brands within this book are for clarifying purposes only and are owned by the owners themselves, not affiliated with this document.

ClydeBank Media LLC is not associated with any organization, product or service discussed in this book. The publisher has made every effort to ensure that the information presented in this book was accurate at time of publication. All precautions have been taken in the preparation of this book. The publisher, author, editor and designer assume no responsibility for any loss, damage, or disruption caused by errors or omissions from this book, whether such errors or omissions result from negligence, accident, or any other cause.

Cover Illustration and Design: Katie Poorman, Copyright © 2015 by ClydeBank Media LLC
Interior Design: Katie Poorman, Copyright © 2015 by ClydeBank Media LLC

ClydeBank Media LLC
P.O Box 6561
Albany, NY 12206

Printed in the United States of America

ClydeBank
MEDIA

Copyright © 2015
ClydeBank Media LLC
www.clydebankmedia.com
All Rights Reserved

ISBN-13 : 978-1511715010

TABLE OF CONTENTS

Introduction 6
    What You'll Need 7
    What You Need to Know 7
    A Note About Versions 7

Chapter 1 : Programming Fundamentals 9
    Constructs 9
    Statements 9
    Functions 10
    Constants and Variables 10
    Scope 12
    Arrays 12
    Operators 12
    Keywords 13
    Expressions 14
    Control Structures 14

Chapter 2 : What Is PHP? 15
    What the Name Means 15
    The Evolution of a Language 15
    What it's Used For 15

Chapter 3 : The Advantages of Using PHP 17

Chapter 4 : PHP Syntax 19
    Beginning and Ending Tags 19
    PHP Statements 20
    Variable Declarations 21
    Comments 22
    Quotes and Strings 24
    Control Structures 27

Chapter 5 : Embedding PHP 29

PHP Document Naming	29
Creating PHP Files	30
Embedded Code Examples	30
Chapter 6 : Building Your First PHP Application	34
Creating the Form	34
Creating the First Control Structure	36
Working with Arrays	37
Testing for Form Submittal	38
Declaring Variables	39
Form Input Validation	39
The Else Condition	41
The Mail Function	41
Controlling HTML Output with PHP	44
Populating Form Fields	46
Chapter 7: Customizing Your PHP Application	49
Glossary	50
Appendix A: PHP Resources	52
Appendix B: Completed Code	53
About ClydeBank Technology	56
More Books by ClydeBank Technology	57

INTRODUCTION

> Terms displayed in ***bold italic*** can be found defined in the glossary on pg. 50.

In today's society, it's hard for most people to imagine life without personal computers and the Internet. Public access to the Internet may be responsible for more changes in the way we carry out our day-to-day lives than any other event in history. Today, businesses without websites are rarities, as are people in the free world that don't spend at least part of their day using the Internet for one purpose or another.

As the demand for websites has grown, website development has become a hobby for some and a profession for many. Today, learning to write Hypertext Markup Language (HTML) and create a web presence is a simple matter, thanks to the availability of hundreds of tutorials available on the subject. Anyone with access to a hosting account can have a basic website up and running in a relatively short time without the need to invest in special software.

Building an *interactive* website, however, often requires more than just HTML code. Enabling features like form processing, database input or output and other functionality means providing programming for those features by means of a web application or "*script*." These scripts can be provided in any of several web-programming languages and are the basis of how visitors interact with websites as well as the "engine" behind ***dynamic websites*** that update content "on the fly."

While it's not limited to web scripting alone, the Hypertext Preprocessor (PHP) language is one of the most popular and widely supported, and it is designed to be almost as easy to learn as HTML and Cascading Style Sheet (***CSS***) coding. It's powerful, versatile and available on almost any hosting network. Like HTML, programming in PHP requires no special software, with the exception of server-side support for the core program.

This guide will provide you with a complete introduction to PHP, from its structure through its basic programming and implementation of simple scripts. After completing this book, you will be able to write your own simple PHP applications and deploy them to add interactivity to your website.

What You'll Need

This book will focus on implementation of PHP scripts on a live *web server.* That means that in order to follow the examples, you'll need a hosting account with PHP 5 support. You'll also need an application that will allow you to edit web page text. That can be a simple text editor such as Notepad, WordPad or Text Edit on your personal computer or a remote application on your *hosting account.*

What You Need to Know

There are a few things you'll need to know to get the most out of this book. While it's written with the novice in mind, you'll need to have a basic set of web developing skills to work with any web-programming language. That means, at the very least, you'll need to need to know how to:

1. *Open, edit and save files on your hosting account*
2. *Make files publicly available*
3. *Enter the correct addresses in your web browser to access those files via the Internet*

File Transfer Protocol, (FTP), web management, HTML coding and other basic techniques are also outside the scope of this book. Let's face it; if you can't write HTML, you won't be able to insert a script into the code, much less tell your script what to output. Please have at least basic skills in those areas before you attempt the lessons herein.

A Note About Versions

At the time of writing, the most current version of PHP is 5.4. Version 7.0 is under development, although a version 6 was never officially released. Version 7.0 will include an upgraded *Zend Engine* that has been proven to significantly improve performance.

Most importantly for the purposes of this text, Version 5.0 introduced an upgrade to the Zend Engine that included an object model to provide support for Object Oriented Programming (**OOP**). While *procedural programming* is still supported, all support for Version 4.0 has been discontinued. Furthermore, although many Version 4.0 scripts are still in use, most hosting companies have removed that functionality. All functions discussed in this book will be taken from Version 5.0 or higher.

CHAPTER ONE
Programming Fundamentals

There are several things you'll need to understand about programming in order to get the greatest benefit from this book. Programming languages differ greatly, but they all share certain traits, and those characteristics are the basis for knowing how to create a program.

This chapter is an introduction to some of the terminology and concepts associated with programming. You'll find many of the terms described in this chapter in the glossary; however, a good grasp of what they mean now will make the following chapters much easier to follow. Let's look at some programming basics.

Constructs

The term "construct" as a noun refers to any assembly of parts of a language that matches the rules of syntax of that language. In English, for instance, the word "a" is a construct. We can use it as-is, because it's a recognizable article of speech.

Constructs in programming languages are basically the same. They may be used independently of other programming elements and are sometimes incorrectly referred to as "commands." It's important to know about constructs because they sometimes don't follow the same rules as other program elements. The "echo" construct is an example we'll use often in our code examples. It causes whatever follows it to be output immediately, normally to the computer screen.

Statements

A statement is the smallest part of a programming language. It's comparable to a sentence in a spoken language, in that it needs to meet certain criteria dictated by the programming language. Statements may identify elements of a program or contain instructions for the computer. A statement may be considered a line of code; however, it's important to realize that PHP statements may span more than one line on a page.

By the same token, multiple PHP statements can be written on the same line of a page.

Functions

A function in a program is a sequence of statements grouped and named with an identifier so that it can be executed from anywhere within the program. By creating functions, a programmer provides an easy way to perform operations without the need to repeat the statements.

Functions may require the input of values when executed. For instance, a program may contain a function that performs math operations on values that must be entered each time the function is executed or "called." In other cases, these values may be parameters limiting the operations of the function. This input is often referred to as "passing" the values. In PHP, values are passed within ***parentheses*** immediately following the name of the function.

Most programming languages, including PHP, include a number of predefined functions and allow for user-defined functions as well.

Constants and Variables

One of the ways we optimize computer programs is by storing values in computer memory for use in various routines within the programs. By storing a value as a block of data, we can use it repeatedly in a program without the need to find its value each time. These "reusable" values are normally stored in one of two ways, as a constant or as a ***variable***.

As the terms imply, the main difference between the two is whether the value of the data can be changed within the program. As you've probably guessed, the value of constants cannot be changed, while variables can be acted on by elements of the program to change the data. Constants are most often used for fixed values that might need to be changed periodically because of some external influence, such as a tax rate. They may also be used to store long strings of text or complex numbers in a way that makes them easier to insert into the program code.

PHP includes several predefined constants, most of which are used for configuring core installations and troubleshooting programming problems. When a variable is stored, extra space is allocated in computer memory to allow for changes.

Since constants can't be changed by the program, only the amount of memory necessary for the original data is used. The data for a constant will also be optimized on the computer for faster access. This saves resources and computing time, also known as "overhead," which is the chief reason to use constants when feasible. PHP constants are created and assigned a value by means of a predefined function: `define`. Constant names are case-sensitive. In other words, "CONSTANT," "Constant" and "constant" would describe three separate names.

PHP Variables are created and assigned their initial values with a statement called a *declaration*. Variable names are also case-sensitive. While any combination of letter case can be used in a variable name, it's good practice to be consistent throughout your programs. *All variable names must begin with the "$" character.*

Each programming language has its own set of rules for declaring variables and constants, as well as the *types* of data allowed. In many programming languages, the **data type** must also be declared. PHP, however, automatically assigns a type to variable and constant data. Names for constants, variables, functions and other elements are considered "labels." Programming languages have rules that determine how valid labels are created. In PHP, labels may contain:

- *Any number of the letters A–Z*
- *Any mix of uppercase and lowercase letters*
- *Any number of underscore (_) characters*

The first character in the label may not be a number; it must begin with a letter or underscore.

> **NOTE**
>
> While there is no rule governing the case used for constant names, the accepted standard is to use all uppercase letters in a constant name, as "CONSTANT." This makes the element clearly identifiable.

> **NOTE**
> PHP constants always have a global scope.

Scope

The scope of a variable, constant or function defines where and how it can be used within a program. Programs, as a rule, have two scopes: local and global. An element with a local scope can only be used within the function where it's declared. Global elements can be used in other areas of the program.

PHP provides an additional scope: static. A variable declared with a static scope has a local scope, but also retains its value when the program flow leaves that scope. For example, a static variable whose value was changed the last time the function containing it was executed, it will have the new value if and when that function is called again.

Arrays

Arrays are special variables that store collections of values and associate a ***key*** or ***index*** with each value stored. Arrays can also be stored as values within arrays. By utilizing arrays, multiple values can be manipulated as a unit. An individual value within an array can be accessed by way of its assigned key or numeric index.

PHP arrays can be created with the `array()` construct. Several predefined arrays also exist within PHP for handing server processes and other actions that may generate a large number of values that can be used in PHP operations.

Operators

If you remember math class, you'll have a basic understanding of what operators are. They're the characters that perform the operations on the elements of a problem. In programming, however, operators can perform many other *operations*. Operators are used to manipulate text, perform logical operations, assign values and much more, in addition to performing all of the math functions you're familiar with. PHP operators can be separated into at least 12 groups for different purposes.

Programming operators, like mathematical operators, have an order of preference. Unlike mathematical operators, however, the preference of a PHP operator in a program doesn't designate order of operations, but how operators are grouped. Complex operations are beyond the scope of this book, but it's important to know that relying on the familiar mathematical order of operations may yield inconsistent results. Parentheses can and should be used to specify the order of operators in complex operations. Operators can also be categorized by their associativity, which determines whether they apply to values on the left, right, or none at all (non-associative). This property also affects grouping, rather than order.

A table of operators showing their preference and associativity can be found in Appendix A.

Keywords

Programming keywords are words that serve a particular purpose in a programming language. They are similar to functions and are often incorrectly referred to as operators or statements, but actually belong in a class of their own and are usually used as building blocks for other program structures. The words "`if`," "`else`" and "`elsif`" are examples common to several programming languages, including PHP.

Using PHP keywords as variable names should be avoided to prevent confusion, and using them as names for constants, functions, classes or methods is not allowed and will cause program errors.

A list of PHP keywords is available under Appendix A.

Expressions

Here's another term you may recognize from math class. An expression is a way to state a value. In other words, you're *expressing* a value in a particular way.

For example, the numeral 3 is an expression of the integer value 3. It can also be expressed as 2 + 1, 14 – 12, 3 * 1, 3/1, "The number of years since my 3-year-old was born," and in countless other ways. That means that almost anything that makes up a program might be considered an expression:

- *A function will return a value.*
- *A declaration assigns a value.*
- *Evaluating a formula returns a value.*
- *A comparison evaluates to TRUE or FALSE.*

Therefore, all of the above are expressions.

Almost everything you write in a PHP program will be an expression. Evaluating those expressions is what makes the program work.

Control Structures

Constructs and statements that control the program flow are referred to as **control structures**. A control structure may specify conditions (*conditional*) or simply tell the program to do something (*instructional*). In most instances, a control structure will determine what happens next by analyzing the data provided to it and applying predetermined rules. These are the elements that help make decisions and perform actions like looping through a series of statements.

PHP includes a very useful and easily understood set of control structures. We'll be using some of them in code examples later.

CHAPTER TWO
What Is PHP?

What the Name Means

When PHP originated in 1994, the acronym represented the term "Personal Home Page." This was because its developer, Rasmus Lerdorf simply created a set of Common Gateway Interface, or ***CGI*** functions written in the C programming language to simplify managing his own web page. Today, after an incredible amount of functionality has been added, the generally accepted meaning of PHP is "Hypertext Preprocessor." This refers to PHP's ability to process the contents of a web page, form or other document before outputting the results to a browser.

The Evolution of a Language

PHP is a ***high-level*** programming language. It shares some syntactical similarities with the C, Perl and Java languages. PHP is open-source software, meaning that the core software can be used, exchanged, modified, and implemented by anyone, free of charge.

One of the many unique things about PHP is that it wasn't conceived as a programming language. Rather, it was originally released to the public as a set of tools for web site maintenance. Forms handling and database functions were added soon after following the formation of a development team, which caused the language to grow at an unprecedented rate. Today, thanks to its open source status, independent developers around the world continue to develop and contributed to it.

What it's Used For

PHP is designed primarily for web applications. However, depending on its implementation, it can be used for desktop applications and more. It's most commonly used for ***server-side*** applications and can be embedded directly in web page code. It can also output HTML code.

One of the most powerful features of PHP is its ability to write to and extract data from online databases. This capability is easily used to create custom web pages on demand and update records via user input. Several modules in the core allow interaction with almost any database software. This feature has been widely used as the basis for several popular Content Management Systems (CMS), including WordPress, Joomla, Drupal and others. It has also been used to create scores of other web-based software packages to handle everything from client and team management to hosting server management.

Web developers use PHP and its modules to create custom applications for websites. In addition to database functions, it can be used to manipulate input and output from web forms, provide information directly from web servers such as date, time, etc. and provide interaction with other sites, such as payment gateways.

CHAPTER THREE
The Advantages of Using PHP

Compared to many other scripting languages, PHP offers several advantages, including, but not limited to:

1. *Wide Support*
Because it's easy to implement, update and maintain, as well as free, PHP is available on the majority of web servers available for public hosting accounts.

2. *No Client-Side Software Required*
Because the **interpreter** runs on the server and PHP doesn't require a **compiler**, you don't need special software to create PHP applications. PHP code can be written in any text application, such as Notepad.

3. *Embedded Code*
PHP code can be embedded directly in HTML code.

4. *Direct Output*
PHP code can output results directly from the code on a page without requiring a fork to an external program. This results in faster execution and less complex programming.

5. *No CGI Required*
Unlike compiled languages, PHP does not require

> **NOTE**
>
> Some web servers use a CGI implementation of the PHP interpreter.

access to a server's CGI. Some hosting companies don't offer this access for security reasons.

6. *Command Line Implementation Optional*

PHP commands can be executed directly from the command line. This allows developers to create server scripts that function without the need for a browser. Developers can use these scripts to access several server functions as well as execute those scripts via the server, for instance, using ***cron*** or Windows Task Scheduler to execute them on a timetable.

7. *Platform Independence*

PHP versions are available for any server and operating system and don't require a web server to run. Developers can even install PHP on their personal computers and run their applications locally.

8. *Services Support*

PHP includes functions that interact with other services on your server of computer. Web services, file transfers, email, and similar services can be accessed directly from your scripts.

9. *Wide Range of Output*

PHP can output much more than just HTML code. You can write images, text, Flash, CSV, PDF and much more directly from your scripts.

10. *Combined Procedural and OOP Support*

PHP supports both procedural and object-oriented programming, allowing developers to use their preferred paradigm.

As previously mentioned, this list is far from all-inclusive. PHP is among the most versatile tools available to web developers, and programmers and independent developers are constantly adding functionality.

CHAPTER FOUR
PHP Syntax

In programming, "syntax" is the term used to describe the rules for how characters are used. Each text-based programming language, like PHP, uses a specific set of characters designated for particular purposes. The syntax of the language determines how those "reserved" characters are used to construct the elements of a program. The most basic of those elements – the building blocks of the programming language - are known as "constructs." In this chapter, we'll examine how those constructs form the basic syntax of PHP.

Beginning and Ending Tags

PHP code is written between beginning and ending constructs called "tags" made up of a specific series of characters. This section will explain how these tags are used.

In a standard PHP environment, the most commonly used format is:

```
<?php somePHPcommand; ?>
```

Or

```
<?php
somePHPcommand;
somePHPcommand;
somePHPcommand;
?>
```

In each of the examples above, "`<?php`" is the beginning tag and "`?>`" is the ending tag. These are the standard tags that enclose a block of PHP code. These 2 tags tell the interpreter on the web server when to start and stop processing the text as PHP

> **NOTE**
>
> Remember that PHP is a pre-processor – the lines of code are processed before being sent to the web browser.

code.

Some web servers may be configured to allow different starting and ending tags. For instance, many will allow the short version of the opening tag: `<?` to be used. Still others may allow Active Server Page (ASP)-style tags: `<% %>`. In many environments, the standard script tags for HTML can be used: `<script language="php">  </script>`. For our purposes, and as a suggested best practice, this book will use the standard tags, as shown in our two examples above.

Keep in mind that when a file contains only PHP code, the ending tag may be omitted. This is often recommended to avoid the output of a newline character. If the PHP code is followed by anything, including comments, HTML or text, the ending tag must be present. The examples in this book will always use the closing tag.

PHP Statements

In PHP, statements must be terminated with a semicolon (;). This makes the semicolon a ***delimiter*** in the PHP language, which is a character that separates types of text.

There is one exception to the semicolon rule, in which the last statement in a function or block of PHP code doesn't require a semicolon.

The PHP interpreter ignores line returns, blank lines and spaces between statements.

The following code block structures are all valid and will produce identical results:

```
<?php statement1;statement2;statement3; ?>
```

```
<?php statement1;   statement2; statement3;   ?>
```

```
<?php
statement1; //(cont'd on next page)
statement2;
statement3;
?>
```

```
<?php
  statement1;
       statement2;
  statement3;
?>
```

This provides great versatility in creating your PHP applications and allows developers to arrange code in ways that make for very easy troubleshooting and general review.

Variable Declarations

As discussed in the previous chapter, PHP variables are created with a declaration statement. We'll be using variables in many of the upcoming code examples, so let's look at how to declare a variable. In PHP, a declaration statement simply contains the variable name (preceded

> **NOTE**
>
> Standards have been developed for consistency in spacing, indenting, and placement of characters in PHP coding. A resource for those standards can be found in Appendix A.

by the "$" sign), followed by an equality sign (=) and the initial value that the variable will represent. (Remember, spaces are ignored in your code, so they can be included for better readability.)

The following are all valid declaration statements:

```php
<?php
$product = 'Little Red Wagon';
$price = 2.95;
$sales_tax = $price * 0.08;
$total = "$".$price + $total;
?>
```

In the preceding code block, note that the value for the first variable, $product, is enclosed in single quotation marks. This tells PHP that the text is to be treated as *string*, which is explained in the following section. What's important to understand in this example is that the spaces in the string will *not* be ignored and are stored as characters in the string.

The second variable contains a numeric value, which we don't enclose in quotes to avoid it being stored as a string. In the third, we perform a mathematical operation; (*) is the multiplication operator on a predefined variable to arrive at the value. In the last, we add the values of 2 variables, using only the variable names in the operation. This illustrates the versatility of variables in PHP.

Comments

Most text-based programming languages allow the use of *comments*, which are lines of text entered strictly for providing information about the code. These lines of text are separated by special delimiters and are ignored by the interpreter when the program runs. Comments are important tools for programmers. They allow:

- *Labels to separate sections of a program*
- *Explanations of program elements*
- *Documentation for other programmers,*

- *Instructions for users of the program,*
- *Notes for themselves, and*
- *Disabling lines of code temporarily for troubleshooting.*

Experienced programmers use comments extensively to simplify the job. They'll be used in our code examples in this book, too, so it's important to recognize them. **Delimiters** are used to separate these comments from executable code. There are three types of comment delimiters in PHP. The code examples below demonstrate how they're used.

Single-line comments can be marked with either the hash character (#) or a pair of slashes (//):

```
<?php //This line won't output anything ?>

<?php #This line won't, either ?>
```

Multi-line comments can also be added. They require an opening delimiter (/*) and a closing delimiter (*/), as below:

```
<?php
/* None of these lines will print.
This is a comment!
So is this.*/
?>
```

Comments can be placed anywhere within code blocks:

```
<?php
echo 'this is a comment'; //this will output the text shown.
# echo 'this is a comment'; //this line will output nothing.
/*
```

The method on the previous page is very handy for disabling one line of code at a time for troubleshooting purposes. As demonstrated in this multi-line comment, you can create as many lines of comments as you like using this method, until you type the ending delimiter, below:

```
*/
echo 'This text will be displayed';
/****** Let's put a comment here ******/
?>
```

Quotes and Strings

In programming, a *string* is a block of text that should be treated as text when the program is executed. In most cases, a string will be output to the display or other device as readable text. Programming languages, such as PHP, use quotation marks (' or ") to differentiate strings from other text. The type of quotation marks used to enclose a block of text is important.

Quotation marks, like those in this text, commonly known as "magic quotes" or "curly quotes" are not used for programming code. Those characters are generated by special character codes. When programming, be certain to set your text editor to use straight quotes (') and (")

In PHP, all strings are **parsed**, meaning that the Zend Engine looks for variables, operators, formulas, etc. within the strings. Quotes give programmers some control over how strings are parsed.

Single Quotes : If a string is enclosed in single quotes ('), it will be considered literal, meaning that operators, etc. won't be evaluated. In other words, the strings will print as they are. There are some exceptions, most notably the single-quote character itself, since it will be interpreted as the end of the string, and the backslash (\) character, since it's the escape character for PHP. To print those characters correctly, they must be preceded by a backslash.

For example:

```
<?php
echo 'Don\'t forget to use a \\ before a backslash.';
?>
```

Double Quotes : Strings enclosed in double quotes (") will have their operators, variables, etc. evaluated when parsed, so values will be substituted. For instance, this code:

```
<?php $chr = 34; echo "This string contains $chr characters." ?>
```

Will print "This string contains 34 characters." If a variable needs to be paired directly with text in this syntax, enclosing it in curly braces will designate where the variable begins and ends:

```
<?php $chr = 'alpha'; echo "This string contains {$chr}numeric characters." ?>
```

The code block above will print, "This string contains alphanumeric characters."

Heredoc and Nowdoc : PHP includes two special types of string syntax that use a special operator (<<<). By using this operator and an identifier, complex, multi-line strings can be printed without the need for complex escaping. The "heredoc" syntax lets you print strings with evaluation. To use this syntax, simply use the operator followed by an identifier that you define, followed by a newline and the string to be parsed. To end the string, type the identifier and a semicolon on a blank line below it.

Please note that this line may not contain any other characters, including any spaces or tabs to indent it.

Here's an example of heredoc syntax:

```
<?php
$a = 'all';
$b = 3;
echo <<<EOS
This string will be printed with $a of its variables evaluated.
Escape characters like the newline above will also be evaluated, so basic
text formatting will be included. (this is line $b)
EOS;
?>
```

The code above will output:

"This string will be printed with all of its variables evaluated.
Escape characters like the newline above will also be evaluated, so basic
text formatting will be included. (this is line 3)"

The "nowdoc" syntax operates identically to heredoc, without evaluation of variables. Unlike strings enclosed in single quotes, strings printed in this syntax do not require escaping of single quotes and backslashes. Using nowdoc syntax is identical to heredoc, except that the identifier is enclosed in single quotes. Here's an example:

```
<?php
$a = 'all';
$b = 3;
echo <<<'EOS'
This string won't require using the \ character.
It will print $a variables exactly as they're typed.
EOS;
?>
```

The previous code will output the following:

"This string won't require using the \ character.
It will print $a variables exactly as they're typed."

These are the basic syntax guidelines for PHP. Syntax for individual elements such as functions, classes, etc. will be covered within the chapters for those elements.

Control Structures

Control structures vary somewhat according to their type and the keywords used to create them. However, there are two basic types of syntax used for creating them. The "standard" syntax is as follows:

```
keyword (parameters) { group of statements }
```

The example above represents only the syntactic elements used to group the portions of the structure. Because PHP allows us to use line breaks, spaces, etc. to organize our code, it's usually more convenient to build the structures like this:

```
keyword (parameters) {
   statement1;
   statement2;
   statement3;
}
```

Again, this is only a basic example of the syntax used to build control structures. Structures may be nested within structures and there will often be multiple options.

For instance, a basic "if/else" structure might look like this:

```
if ($roses == 'red') {
   if ($violets == 'blue') {
      echo 'Sugar is sweet';
   } else {
      echo 'Violets are purple';
   }
}
```

If the code above doesn't make sense to you yet, don't worry; we'll go over these structures many times in the upcoming pages. For now, just focus on the way the parameters of the control and the instructional statements are grouped.

As previously mentioned, this is one of two choices of syntax for most control structures. The "alternate" syntax is shown in the example below, using the same control structure as above:

```
   if ($roses == 'red') :
      if ($violets == 'blue') :
         echo 'Sugar is sweet';
      endif;
   else :
      echo 'Violets are purple';
   endif;
```

Note that the curly braces ({ }) have been replaced with a colon (:) and another keyword, "endif." Otherwise, the structure remains the same. This syntax lends itself well to some applications. It's also the basis for a "shortcut" syntax, and we'll cover both of those topics in the next chapter.

CHAPTER FIVE
Embedding PHP

In this chapter you'll start using some of what you've been learning and will begin to write PHP code. If you've read the last 3 chapters, you should be just about ready to dive in.

PHP can be embedded in HTML code in several different ways. Developers can mix embedding methods within the same document, as needed. It's important to note that code can be embedded *anywhere* within a document, even inside the opening and closing brackets of an HTML tag. This allows developers to create conditional attributes for HTML elements within their documents, among other things.

PHP code is executed separately from HTML code and isn't subject to the rules of the HTML structure. That means that the PHP code can also be located anywhere within the document and can be written in separate documents and called with the `include` and `require` functions as needed within the HTML. In the latter cases, the code will be executed as if it resided within the current page, providing a way for functions or other blocks of PHP code to be made available to an entire site without the need to continually rewrite them.

PHP Document Naming

The examples we're about to create will be ready to run on a live web server. There's one more important consideration, and that's how the server recognizes a document that contains PHP code. The PHP code will need to be ***parsed*** by the PHP interpreter in order to run. Otherwise, it will be delivered to the browser as HTML and will probably create errors that will make the document unreadable.

Web servers differ in the way they recognize documents that contain executable code (programs). The standard method is to pass any document with a file name that ends in ".php" to the PHP interpreter. That's the standard we'll be using in this book. If you're unsure of how your web host handles PHP files, please contact your hosting

Creating PHP Files

If you're already using a software application to create web pages, chances are you'll be able to use it to create PHP files. If not, you can use a text editor like NotePad, WordPad or Simple Text to write your code.

When saving files, many text editors automatically add a default file extension. The most commonly used is ".txt". In some cases, that extension can't be replaced with ".php". If your editor does this, simply save the "myfile.php.txt" and remove the ".txt" later, either on your computer or on the web server.

Embedded Code Examples

The following series of examples will demonstrate the most common ways to directly embed PHP code in an HTML document. In the first example, we'll show how a variable can be created anywhere in a document and used in the body:

```
<?php $myname = 'John Doe'; // variable declaration?>
<html>
<head>
<title>PHP Programming Example 1</title>
</head>
<body>
Hello, my name is <?php echo $myname; ?>.
</body>
</html>
```

In the preceding example, the PHP code is in **bold** type for easy identification. As you can see, we've created a variable named "myname" and assigned it an initial value of "John Doe." That operation will be performed even before the opening HTML tag is output. Within the body of the document, we've used the echo construct to output the value of the variable directly in line with a string of text being output to the browser.

The blocks of PHP code are opened and closed separately. Starting and stopping PHP code in this way is a feature you'll learn to use to your advantage in many ways. In many cases, such as using PHP to manipulate browser cookies, the PHP code MUST be written before the opening HTML tag. It's also common to write complex functions at the top of the document to speed up output when the page starts to load to the browser.

Type the code above into your editor and save the file with the name "myfile.php" and upload it to the public folder on your hosting account. Open your browser and point it to (your web address)/myfile.php. If everything is correctly typed and configured, your browser window should read, "Hello, my name is John Doe." on your screen. If so, congratulations! You've just written and executed your first PHP program. There won't be any fancy formatting, but we'll get to that soon.

Note that if your web page doesn't perform as expected, carefully check your code, making sure you've entered all the semicolons, opening and closing tags, and other characters exactly the way they appear in the book. You may also need to verify that your file name is correct and ends in ".php". If you still have trouble getting the correct results after taking the steps above, check your hosting account to make sure that PHP is available and configured correctly. Don't continue with the following examples until this page works as described. When your first PHP program runs correctly, you can move on to the next example.

As previously mentioned, there are multiple ways to embed PHP code in a document. In the example below, you'll see that the PHP code has been condensed into one block in the body of the document. You'll also notice that the `echo` statement now contains all of the text we want to output, enclosed in double quotes.

You may recall that by enclosing a string in double quotes, we tell the PHP interpreter that it should perform any operations found. The "$" character tells the interpreter to treat the text after it as a variable and output its current value, in this case, "John Doe."

```
<html><head><title>PHP Programming Example 2</title></head>
<body>
<?php
$myname = 'John Doe'; // variable declaration
echo "Hello, my name is $myname.";
?>
</body>
</html>
```

If you save this block of code as a PHP file and upload it to your account, you should see exactly the same results as the previous file when you open it in your browser. It's quite common to embed large blocks of PHP code in the HTML body. It's also possible to embed HTML code within PHP code, in a manner of speaking. This can be very convenient for displaying HTML without the need to use complex echo statements. Here's an example using an if/else construct:

```
<?php if ($a == 1){ ?>
   <a href="page1.html">Go to Page 1</a>
<?php } else { ?>
   <strong>PLEASE SELECT A PAGE</strong>
<?php } ?>
```

Note that the PHP code in the example above is simply opened and closed at the beginning and ending brackets for the control structure. Since the PHP interpreter stops evaluating code between the closing and opening tags, the output to the browser in those areas will be sent as HTML.

Although the example above will work fine, this is one instance in which readability can be improved by using the alternate control structure syntax, as below:

```php
<?php if ($a == 1): ?>
  <a href="page1.html">Go to Page 1</a>
<?php else: ?>
  <strong>PLEASE SELECT A PAGE</strong>
<?php endif; ?>
```

Using either of the methods above is extremely convenient when a PHP control structure is used to control large blocks of HTML code. Up to now, we've used very basic code examples to give you a foothold on the process of programming in PHP. Now that you're familiar with the basics, we'll move on in the following chapters to create a useful PHP application to run on your website.

CHAPTER SIX
Building Your First PHP Application

The previous chapters have given you all the information you need to write programs in PHP and embed them in web pages. In this chapter, we'll begin creating a working application with an HTML form and a PHP program that processes the information it collects. You'll be creating a basic contact form, useful for ensuring that website owners collect the information necessary to respond to viewers.

As you build the application, you'll learn how to:

- Work with arrays in PHP,
- Import form input as PHP variables,
- Validate form input with PHP,
- Output PHP variable values with "shortcut" code,
- Use PHP to preload values for form inputs,
- Use PHP to determine which HTML to display to a web browser,
- Use PHP to run services on a web server, and
- **Concatenate** strings in PHP.

Creating the Form

Let's start by creating the basic form. The code block on the following page contains the form with which we'll start. If you're an HTML expert, you'll notice that the page code is very basic. Once you've completed the application and tested it on your website, you may want to add meta tags, etc. as needed for your site. For the purposes of this project, basic HTML will be less confusing.

Copy the code block below to a file and save it as contactform.php.

```html
<!DOCTYPE HTML PUBLIC "-//W3C//DTD HTML 4.01 Transitional//EN" "http://www.w3.org/TR/html4/loose.dtd">
<html>
<head>
<meta http-equiv="Content-Type" content="text/html; charset=iso-8859-1">
<title>Contact Form</title>
</head>
<body>
<p>If you have questions about this site, please use the form below to contact us, so that we can provide the best possible answers.</p>
<p> Fields with <strong>bold</strong> labels are required.</p>
<form method="post" action="contactform.php">
<strong>First Name</strong> 
<input type="text" name="fname" size="20"><br>
<strong>Last Name</strong> 
<input type="text" name="lname" size="20"><br>
Phone 
<input type="text" name="phone" size="20"><br>
<strong>Email Address</strong> 
<input type="text" name="fname" size="20"><br>
<strong>Type your question below:</strong><br>
<textarea name="msg" cols="50" rows="10"></textarea><br>
<input type="submit" name="submit" value="Send">
</body>
</html>
```

Once you've created the new file, go ahead and make it available on your website. Open it in your browser and verify that there are no problems.

There's no need to analyze the HTML code in great detail; the form itself is standard. You'll be making modifications and additions as we proceed. You'll want to note two things about the <form> tag:

1. The form method is "post." This will be important to our PHP program.
2. The form action is "contactform.php", which means that the form will be calling the same page on which it resides. Your PHP code will be intelligent enough to determine what action to take when this page is delivered to your browser. This application will be entirely self-contained, all on a single web page!

One more unusual feature on this form is the "name" attribute on the submit button, which is often omitted on an HTML form. This attribute will be important to our application.

Creating the First Control Structure

Now we're ready to start writing PHP code. The first block of code we're going to create will be placed above everything else on the page. That means that when the web server receives a request for contactform.php, it will read that code before sending anything to the browser. This is important for 2 reasons:

1. Web servers and browsers send important information about pages back and forth in data blocks called Hypertext Transfer Protocol (HTTP) headers. The headers are passed before any other information and can only be sent once per request. Because PHP often uses these headers to control certain processes, it's important that the PHP code be placed on the page above the HTML tags, which signal the end of a header.
2. The PHP control structure we'll be writing at this stage will determine how the page is displayed each time the page is accessed.

The first items we'll need are the opening and closing tags for this block of code. Getting into the habit of creating these tags first in order to "set up your work space" will help you avoid errors. We're going to be writing many lines of code in this block, so at the top of your contactform.php file, add these three lines:

```
<?php


?>
```

Again, be sure to place this block of code at the absolute top of the document. You'll start writing on the blank line in the center. Placing your opening and closing tags this way give you an easy way to find where your PHP code begins and ends later.

Since this program will process the input from the form on our page, we'll need to know whether the form has been submitted when the page loads. (Remember – when a visitor submits the form, the information is sent to this same page.) Let's start by learning how PHP recognizes the input from the form.

Working with Arrays

When a form is submitted on a web page, it sends an HTTP request header to the web server. Along with other information, the header will contain all of the form input field names and the value that was input for each. When the PHP interpreter, remember, this is a PHP page, so it's passed to the interpreter, encounters these inputs, it creates an array of those values, with a special name. Since the form on our page is using the "post" method, the name for the array will be `$_POST`.

To use a value from a PHP array, we can refer to it directly using its numeric index (position in the array)

> **NOTE**
>
> The `$_` character sequence is an important one in PHP that designates a predefined (built-in) variable. To avoid confusion, it's best not to use this sequence for your own variable names.

> **NOTE**
>
> The single quotes around the label inside the brackets, designating the name as a literal text string. If a variable is used to represent the key, the quotes should be omitted.

or its label. The values sent from a form will be assigned keys matching the "name" attributes of the HTML input tags of the form. These variables and the array itself are also assigned a type of "superglobal," meaning they can be used anywhere in a PHP program.

The syntax for getting the value of an array element by key is:

```
array name[key].
```

Thus, the following code: `$_POST['fname']` will return the value of the "fname" field in our form. Each input in the form can be read directly into our program in this way.

Testing for Form Submittal

Let's create the code that determines what to do if the form has been submitted. We'll do this with an "if" control structure and a built-in PHP function: `isset`. Here's the code:

```
/*** if the form was submitted, get the input values ***/
    if (isset($_POST['submit'])) {
      $fname = $_POST['fname'];
      $lname = $_POST['lname'];
      $phone = $_POST['phone'];
      $email = $_POST['email'];
      $msg = $_POST['msg'];
    } //end the if construct
```

Note the comments added to clarify each step. Now, let's analyze what this code block does. First, we use the `isset` function to test whether the submit button was clicked. You'll recall that we gave that button a name in the HTML code. Our "if" construct tests to see if that name has been set, in other words, whether it exists for our program.

If the submit button was clicked, the button's name will be set and the instructions within the curly braces will be executed. If not, everything within the braces will be ignored and the program will simply move ahead to the next statement.

Declaring Variables

Assuming the form was submitted, our program now assigns simple variable names to each form input value except the submit button, which won't we need for anything else. *Note that the single equal sign (=) is an assignment operator, used to assign values, rather than to compare them.*

Add the code from the block above to your contactform.php code. *This is a complete control structure.*

Form Input Validation

Now, before we do anything else with the values, remember that we told the visitors that some inputs are required. We can use PHP to "validate" the form input, ensuring that those required fields are filled. To do this, we'll "nest" an "if" control structure inside the one we just completed.

Since we've declared variables for each input, we can now use those variable names instead of the more complex array elements to simplify working with those values. To check each of the required variables, we'll use another built-in function: empty. This function returns a **Boolean** value of TRUE if a variable name has a null value.

Here's the code we'll add to perform the validation procedure:

```
/*** test for required inputs ***/
if (empty($fname) || empty($lname) ||
   empty($email) || empty($msg)) {
     $error = TRUE;
}
```

Let's analyze the code block above. First of all, note that the first line of code has been wrapped midway through the parameters to make it easier to read. PHP allows line wrapping between quotes, parentheses, etc. Second, we're introducing a new operator in this code block. *The double pipe character (||) is the logical OR operator.*

Read aloud, this block of code says, "If $fname is empty or $lname is empty or $email is empty or $msg is empty, then create $error and make it TRUE." That's the procedure it performs, so if any of the required fields are empty, there will be an error message that we can use later. *Note the lack of quotes around the word TRUE. This syntax assigns a Boolean value of TRUE rather than the string "TRUE."*

We'll want to perform this test only if the form is submitted, so this code will need to be within the first "if" structure we created. Copy it into your file just below the last line in the structure and above the closing curly brace (}). Leave the leading spaces as they are in the code block, to make the program flow easier to trace.

So far, we've checked to see if the form was submitted, and if so, checked to see if all of the required

NOTE

This is very basic form validation. If a field contains any characters, including the space character, the empty function will return FALSE. More complex validation can be performed with PHP, but that is beyond the scope of this book.

input was submitted. We then defined an error message we can use if any input is missing.

Now it's time to tell the interpreter what we want to do with the information if we have it all. Although there are many options, we're going to use a very convenient and sophisticated built-in PHP function to send the information to you by email.

The Else Condition

First, the way in which we determine whether to move to the next step will introduce you to the beauty of the "if/else" construct. Up to this point, our script (program) says, "If the form has been submitted, get the input values and see if any of the required ones are empty. If any are empty, create $error and make it true." Now, if none of the required input values are empty, we'll do something "else."

To create the new "else" conditional statement, we simply add the term to the closing bracket of the "if" with which we're concerned and add another set of braces. Here's how it will look with our last block:

```
/*** test for required inputs ***/
if (empty($fname) || empty($lname) ||
  empty($email) || empty($msg)) {
  $error = TRUE;
} else {
} //end if/else construct
```

The obvious next step is to create the instructions for the else condition. In this case, we've run our tests and we're ready to create and send an email containing the information from the form. We'll do that with a built-in PHP function that sends commands to the web server's email service, i.e. the programs that send and receive email. The function name is mail.

The Mail Function

In order to easily provide the mail function with all the necessary parameters, we'll declare some variables and assign the message information as values. While we're at it, you'll learn how to use two new operators. We'll start with a couple of straightforward variables:

```
/*** send email ***/
$recipient = 'me@mydomain.com';
$subject = 'Website contact';
```

Change 'me@mydomain.com' to your own email address in the above code.

Next, we'll build the body of the email message, the part you'll read, one line at a time, using a special operator known as the *concatenating assignment operator*. This operator, also known as the "dot equal" sign (. =), tells the interpreter that the left string should now be equal to the left string followed by the right string. This makes it very easy to assign long strings to a variable name, as we'll do here:

```
$body = "The following message was sent";
$body .= "via your website contact form:\n\n";
$body .= "Name: $fname $lname\n";
$body .= "Email: $email\n";
if (empty($phone) == FALSE) {
   $body .= "Phone: $phone\n";
}
$body .= "\n$msg";
```

In the code above, we started with a variable declaration and assigned it a string value. On the next line, we used the dot equal operator to add another string to the same variable. If we'd used the equal sign, the second string would have replaced the first. Using the (=) assignment operator on a variable that already has a value will reassign it using the new value.

Note also that we've used double quotes on these strings. This tells the interpreter to evaluate any operators in the strings and use the value of variables instead of the literal text. You'll see where the variable names for the form input values have been entered. Notice also the escaped "n" character (\n), which will print a "newline" character to create a line break in your email message.

Lastly, notice the "if" construct we've used to determine whether the visitor provided a phone number and add it to the message. Most importantly, note the double equal sign operator inside the parentheses. This operator is a *comparator* that checks for equality between the left and right values. We've used the empty function again here, but in this case, we want to verify that the variable contains a value, meaning the empty function will return FALSE.

In the last line of the code block, we add the value of the `<textarea>` element of the HTML form, completing the body of the email.

The next step in preparing the email is to create a set of headers required by the server and the receiving email client program. We'll use the same basic method as was used to create the email body:

```
$headers = "From: webform@mydomain.com\r\n";
$headers .= "Reply-to: $email\r\n\r\n";
```

Change "mydomain.com" to your domain name in the above code.

This completes the process of preparing the information required by the mail function. Now we can provide the information as parameters in the function call quite easily, using the variables we've created. At the same time, we'll create a test procedure to ensure that the email is sent to the server and our mailing application completed successfully:

```
$sent = (mail($recipient, $subject, $body, $headers));
if ($sent) {
  $success = TRUE;
}
```

These blocks of code complete the programming we need to do before the HTML output begins, and the next line on the page should contain only the PHP closing tag we added earlier. Save your file again.

Controlling HTML Output with PHP

In addition to sending the form input by email, the script we created in the top of the document created all the elements we need to determine what our page will display each time it's requested. Why would we want to do that? To customize what the visitor sees in response to what action was taken.

In this case, we're going to first present the visitor with the contact form. When the form is submitted, we'll do one of these two things:

1. Present the form again, *with the information that was submitted in place*, along with an error message if required information is missing
2. Present a nice thank you page if the send was successful

We'll be able to do all of that without sending the visitor to another page simply by using a PHP control structure to determine some of the HTML output. We'll be writing our code in the HTML body and using the alternate control structure syntax described earlier in the book to simplify mixing the HTML and PHP.

On the following page, you'll find the original HTML body with some PHP code blocks added. The PHP code is in bold type for clarity. HTML comments have also been added to help identify the sections of the page.

```
<body>
<?php if ($success): ?>
<!-- EMAIL SENT. PRINT THANK YOU PAGE -->
<?php else: ?>
<!-- EMAIL NOT SENT. FORM NOT SUBMITTED OR INPUT MISSING -->
  <?php if ($error): ?>
<!-- INPUT MISSING. DISPLAY ERROR MESSAGE -->
  <?php endif; ?>
<!-- PRINT THE FORM -->
<p>If you have questions about this site, please use the form
```

```
below to contact us, so that we can provide the best possible
answers.</p>
    <p> Fields with <strong>bold</strong> labels are required.</p>
    <form method="post" action="contactform.php">
    <strong>First Name</strong> 
    <input type="text" name="fname" size="20"><br>
    <strong>Last Name</strong> 
    <input type="text" name="lname" size="20"><br>
    Phone 
    <input type="text" name="phone" size="20"><br>
    <strong>Email Address</strong> 
    <input type="text" name="fname" size="20"><br>
    <strong>Type your question below:</strong><br>
    <textarea name="msg" cols="50" rows="10"></textarea><br>
    <input type="submit" name="submit" value="Send">
    <?php endif; ?>
    </body>
```

All we need to do now is add the HTML code we want to display for each condition. Let's start with the "Thank you" message. We'll want the visitor to see this message after the email is successfully sent. Consulting our PHP code, you'll see that when the send was successful, we created a variable named "success" and gave it a Boolean value of TRUE. Our first "if" statement checks that variable.

Note that `if($success)` means the same thing as `if($success= TRUE)`. *When testing a Boolean value, it's not necessary to use the longer version.*

Let's create a simple message to let the visitor know the operation was a success:

```
    <div style="margin:auto; text-align:center">
    <h2>Thank you for contacting us!</h2>
    Your email has been sent and we'll respond as quickly as
possible.
    </div>
```

Place the HTML code above on your page, directly underneath the first HTML comment and above `<?php else: ?>`.

Next, let's create an error message:

```
<div style="font-weight:bold; color:#ff0000;">
Please enter input for each field with a <strong>bold</strong>label.
</div>
```

This error message should be placed on your page directly under this HTML comment tag:

```
<!-- INPUT MISSING. DISPLAY ERROR MESSAGE -->
```

That's it! Your page now has everything needed to display HTML code customized to suit each condition.

Populating Form Fields

Now, let's add one more feature. If you've tested your application, and it's working correctly, you'll notice that, if one of the required inputs is missing, it prints an error message, but all the other information that *was* entered has disappeared. That means that your visitor is going to have to provide that information again.

What if there was a way to preserve that information in the newly displayed form? Fortunately, there is! You'll recall that PHP code can be embedded *anywhere* within an HTML document. We can take advantage of that fact by using the `echo` construct to place the value of the variables we created from the previous inputs in the "value" attribute of our form fields. This is known as *populating* the form fields.

Let's use another convenient PHP feature to make this process easier. There's a "shortcut" for the echo construct that works nicely for this kind of operation. Instead of typing:

```
<?php echo "something" ?>,
```

We can use:

```
<?= "something" ?>
```

To accomplish the same thing. Here's how it looks with the first of our HTML input tags on the form:

```
<input type="text" name="fname" size="20" value="<?= $fname ?>">
```

By adding this to each of the input fields on our form using the appropriate variable names, the information your visitor entered before submitting the form will still be there if the form is displayed again. If a form field was left blank, it will, of course, be blank.

If you're wondering, *"What about the text for the message?"*, good thinking. This form field has to be treated a little differently, but it's still a simple matter. The HTML `<textarea>` tag is a "container" tag that requires a closing tag: `</textarea>`. Anything that's typed between the two tags will be displayed in the text box on the form.

> **NOTE**
>
> Variable names aren't enclosed in quotes when we want to display their values. Using quotes around the name will cause the interpreter to print the name as a string.

To place the previously-entered text there, we simply use the shortcut tag to print the value of that variable between them:

```
<textarea name="msg" cols="50" rows="10">
    <?= $msg ?>
</textarea>
```

Now that your form is populated for the error routine, your application is complete. Make it available on your hosting account and test it thoroughly. If you encounter errors, go back to the beginning of this chapter and check each step in turn.

In addition, it's important to know that differences in email servers may cause unexpected issues with the PHP mail function. If your application appears to work correctly, but you're not receiving the email, first make sure you've entered the email address correctly and then check with your hosting service on how to use remote commands for the email server.

> **NOTE**
>
> If you continue to experience problems with your application, use the code provided in Appendix B in a new file to test its compatibility with your host's web server. If that page does not work correctly, chances are there is a compatibility problem. In this case, contact your host's documentation or technical support staff for advice on overcoming the issues.

CHAPTER SEVEN
Customizing Your PHP Application

Congratulations! By now, you should have a complete, working contact page for your website visitors. You've also learned the basics of PHP programming and how to use it in your web pages to create dynamic applications. Now that you have a working application in place, you can customize the text for your messages to suit your own taste and the needs of your site.

You can, of course, put your HTML and CSS skills to work to make the display blend with your website. You may want to gather more information from your visitors, such as gender, age, etc. The purpose of your website will no doubt determine what information is important for you to have. Not all HTML form elements are alike, so if you want to add radio buttons, checkboxes or other features, you may need to do a little research to determine how PHP works with those elements. Fortunately, documentation is readily available from the resources listed in Appendix A.

Although this book has provided only an introduction into the world of PHP programming, you should, by now, realize that this extremely powerful programming language is also easier to use than you may have thought. With no special software required and simple, text-based programming, there may be no better way to create dynamic, powerful applications for your websites.

As outlined in Chapter 2, PHP offers a host of advantages over other programming languages, not the least of which is ease of learning. With the basic skills you've learned in this text and the resources listed in the appendices, you should find the transition from web designer to programmer an easy one.

GLOSSARY

Boolean -
In reference to a program variable, one that has a binary value of TRUE or FALSE.

CGI - Common Gateway Interface, a web server interface that allows hosted content to interact with programs stored on the server. Typically used for implementation of applications written in C, Perl, Java and similar languages.

Concatenate -
to join elements together to form a series or chain, particularly strings.

Constant -
A fixed value cataloged for use in a program and assigned a label, which is used to reference the value for the program. The value of a constant remains the same throughout the program.

Control Structure -
A group of program statements that determines program flow by analyzing data provided and acting according to predetermined parameters.

Cascading Style Sheets (CSS)-
Rules that define a website's look and feel.

Compiler -
A software application that converts high-level code into binary code executable by a computer.

Cron -
A built-in program on Unix-style web servers that can be used to execute stored programs at timed intervals.

Delimiter -
A character or series of characters designated for the separation of various types of text in a programming language.

Dynamic Website -
A website that delivers content that may vary in response to user input, date, time, or other conditions.

High-level -
Denotes a programming language that does not require the programmer to write machine-readable code in order to create working applications.

Hosting Account -
An account and the associated disk space allotted to the client of a hosting company, normally used to store the content for the client's website.

Index -
The numeric position of an element in a PHP array. PHP array indexing begins at zero.

Interpreter -
A software application that converts high-level code into an intermediate code before conversion to binary code executable by a computer.

Key -
The label applied to an element in an associative array. Associative arrays consist of key and value pairs, wherein the key can be used to reference the value.

OOP (Object Oriented Programming) -
A programming method based on instances of objects and their classes and methods, to approximate real-world situations.

Parentheses -
A pair of parenthetical signs, as ( ), used to contain parameters for a PHP statement.

Parse -
The act of analyzing a string of text and interpreting its elements to produce the desired result. In PHP, parsing is accomplished by the language's built-in interpreter in order to execute the programming code.

Procedural Programming -
A programming method in which procedures are created by means of a step-by-step series of statements that return a result.

Script -
A web application, i.e. a program intended to run on an internet site.

Server-side -
Refers to an application that runs on a web server to deliver content to a web browser or other remote software. Server-side code offers transparency and saves resources on client computers as compared to client-side.

Variable -
A non-fixed value cataloged for use in a program, assigned a label which is used to reference the value during a program. The value of a variable can be acted upon and changed by statements within the program.

Web Server -
A software application that resides on a computer connected to the Internet, designed to deliver website content in response to requests from "client" applications such as web browsers.

Zend Engine -
The name given to the PHP interpreter included as part of the core software.

APPENDIX A

PHP Resources

PHP Operators:
http://php.net/manual/en/language.operators.php

PHP Keywords:
http://php.net/manual/en/reserved.keywords.php

PHP Coding Practices:
http://en.wikibooks.org/wiki/PHP_Programming/Coding_Standards#PHP_Syntax

APPENDIX B

Completed Code

```php
<?php
/*** if the form was submitted, get the input values ***/
if (isset ($_POST['sendbutton'])) {
  $fname = $_POST['fname'];
  $lname = $_POST['lname'];
  $phone = $_POST['phone'];
  $email = $_POST['email'];
  $msg = $_POST['msg'];
  /*** test for required inputs ***/
  if (empty($fname) || empty($lname) ||
    empty($email) || empty($msg)) {
    $error = TRUE;
  } else {
    /*** send email ***/
    $recipient = 'me@mydomain.com'; //set to your email
    $subject = 'Website contact';
    $body = "The following message was sent";
    $body .= "via your website contact form:\n\n";
    $body .= "Name: $fname $lname\n";
    $body .= "Email: $email\n";
    if (empty($phone) == FALSE) {
      $body .= "Phone: $phone\n";
    }
    $body .= "\n$msg";
    $headers = "From: webform@mydomain.com\r\n";
```

```php
        //change mydomain.com to your domain
        $headers .= "Reply-to: $email\r\n\r\n";
        $sent = (mail($recipient, $subject, $body, $headers));
        if ($sent) {
          $success = TRUE;
        }  // end the if construct
      }  //end the if/else construct
    }  //end the if construct
    ?>
```

```html
    <!DOCTYPE HTML PUBLIC "-//W3C//DTD HTML 4.01 Transitional//EN"
"http://www.w3.org/TR/html4/loose.dtd">
    <html>
    <head>
    <meta http-equiv="Content-Type" content="text/html; charset=iso-8859-1">
    <title>Contact Form</title>
    </head>
    <body>
    <?php if ($success): ?>
    <!-- EMAIL SENT. PRINT THANK YOU PAGE →
    <div style="margin: auto; text-align:center">
    <h2>Thank you for contacting us!</h2>
    Your email has been sent and we'll respond as quickly as possible.
    </div>
    <?php else: ?>
    <!-- EMAIL NOT SENT. FORM NOT SUBMITTED OR INPUT MISSING →
    <?php if ($error): ?>
    <!-- INPUT MISSING. DISPLAY ERROR MESSAGE →
    <div style="font-weight:bold; color:#ff0000;">
    Please enter input for each field with a <strong>bold</strong>label.
```

```html
		</div>
		<?php endif; ?>
	<p>If you have questions about this site, please use the form below to contact us, so that we can provide the best possible answers.</p>
		<p> Fields with <strong>bold</strong> labels are required.</p>
		<form method="post" action="./contactform.php">
		<strong>First Name</strong> 
		<input type="text" name="fname" size="20" value="<?= $fname ?>"><br>
		<strong>Last Name</strong> 
		<input type="text" name="lname" size="20" value="<?= $lname ?>"><br>
		Phone 
		<input type="text" name="phone" size="20" value="<?= $phone ?>"><br>
		<strong>Email Address</strong> 
		<input type="text" name="email" size="20" value="<?= $email ?>"><br>
		<strong>Type your question below:</strong><br>
		<textarea name="msg" cols="50" rows="10"><?= $msg ?></textarea><br>
		<input type="submit" name="sendbutton" value="Send">
		<?php endif; ?>
	</body>
</html>
```

ABOUT
CLYDEBANK TECHNOLOGY

ClydeBank Technology is a division of the multimedia-publishing firm ClydeBank Media LLC. ClydeBank Media's goal is to provide affordable, accessible information to a global market through different forms of media such as eBooks, paperback books and audio books. Company divisions are based on subject matter, each consisting of a dedicated team of researchers, writers, editors and designers.

The Technology division of ClydeBank Media is composed of contributors who are experts in their given disciplines. Contributors originate from diverse areas of the world to guarantee the presented information fosters a global perspective. Contributors have multiple years of experience in IT systems, networking, programming, web development and design, database development and management, graphic design and many other areas of discipline.

>For more information, please visit us at
>**www.clydebankmedia.com**
>or email us at
>**contact info@clydebankmedia.com**

MORE BOOKS BY CLYDEBANK TECHNOLOGY

WordPress Mastery
Exactly How To Become A WordPress Expert & Create Profitable Websites & Blogs In Minutes
URL : bit.ly/wordpress_mastery

Evernote Mastery
Exactly How To Use Evernote To Organize Your Life, Manage Your Day & Get Things Done
URL : bit.ly/evernote_mastery

Raspberry Pi For Beginners
Everything You Need To Know To Get The Most Out of Your Raspberry Pi
URL : bit.ly/rapberrypi

SQL Quickstart Guide
The Ultimate Beginner's Guide To Learning SQL
URL : bit.ly/learn_SQL

ITIL For Beginners
The Complete Beginner's Guide To ITIL
URL : bit.ly/learn_ITIL

GET A FREE CLYDEBANK MEDIA AUDIOBOOK
+ 30 DAY FREE TRIAL TO AUDIBLE.COM

GET TITLES LIKE THIS ABSOLUTELY FREE:

- *Business Plan Writing Guide*
- *ITIL for Beginners*
- *Stock Options for Beginners*
- *Scrum Quickstart Guide*
- *Project Management for Beginners*
- *3D Printing Business*
- *LLC Quickstart Guide*
- *Lean Six Sigma Quickstart Guide*
- *Growing Marijuana for Beginners*
- *Social Security Simplified*
- *Medicare Simplified*
- and more!

TO SIGN UP & GET YOUR FREE AUDIOBOOK, VISIT:
www.clydebankmedia.com/audible-trial

Made in the USA
Middletown, DE
06 June 2016